Hugo

from

Toots

Christmas 2019

THE LION

Our lion is one of six surviving medieval lions which, standing proudly
on plinths, once decorated a great mansion in Cornwall. They are
carved out of moorstone granite, had heraldic shields painted on their
chests and may now be some six hundred years old. Of the six known
lions, the National Trust has two at Trerice and two at Glendurgan.
The other two are at the home of the author.

Stephen Tyrrell is a historian and writer on architectural
history and lives in Cornwall. He has written some dozen books and
edited others.

First Edtion 2019
Text, artwork, drawings design and presentation
copyright Pasticcio and S C S Tyrrell
Set in Bell MT 11 on 13.2; headings in Aleo
Published by Pasticcio, a division of F. Smyth-Tyrrell & Co Ltd.
Registered (1981) in England No 1532428
01326 340153   www.pasticcio.co.uk
ISBN 978-0-9570311-2-8

Pasticcio

Publishers

FANCIFUL FOLLIES
& IMPROBABLE BUILDINGS

Stephen Tyrrell

ACKNOWLEDGEMENTS

After a lifetime spent renovating interesting structures for clients, I thank those clients for their support, despite their resolute refusal to build the flights of the ridiculous which I have suggested. Although their buildings may, therefore, have remained sensible and safe, I still believe that the world has thereby lost some fascinating fancies.

It is also proper to give thanks to my family, despite their opinion that I should be walled up in one of the more secure creations on these pages.

No review of unusual buildings should fail to acknowledge the works of Osbert Lancaster and Heath Robinson.

We would love to have thanked a sponsor, but were unable to find anyone fool enough to back the project.

SOURCES AND READING LIST

The following books have proved useful for the checking of references:

WC Sellar & RJ Yeatman: 1066 & All That. *Methuen & Co 1930*
Heath Robinson & KRG Browne: How to live in a Flat. *Hutchinson & Co 1936*
Osbert Lancaster: Draynefleet Revealed. *John Murray 1949*
Osbert Lancaster: A Cartoon History of Architecture. *John Murray 1959 & 1975*

IMPORTANT NOTICE

This illustrated book requires leaps of the imagination. In accordance with health and safety legislation, users should be aware that, although some exercise is considered good for health, such leaps should only be undertaken with adult supervision.

The book should not be read by those under 65 years of age.

This book may contain moving parts which, individually, could cause harm.

Neither this product nor its content are thought likely to contain or cause an allergic reaction.

CONTENTS

continued

INTRODUCTION

This book of sketches cheerfully mixes the odd fact with frivolous fantasy. The drawings are not always of real buildings and the accompanying text should be read with caution. It is not always serious.

A few of the pages started life as cards sent to those who enjoyed building renovation. They had an architectural context and often referred, even if obliquely, to a project completed that year. The earlier sketches had a Cornish slant because that is where I live. Many drawings continue to include some allusion to Christmas.

This is therefore a selection of imagined structures, but although they are only imaginary, reality demonstrates that no imagined structures can live up to what man can create. Follies and unusual buildings, space age adventures, archaeology, science fiction and computer games have all demonstrated that it is difficult for our imagination to keep up with reality. Follies, which are buildings with no practical purpose, are so popular that there are hundreds in Britain alone; the Folly Fellowship lists numerous books on these idiotic buildings, including some forty follies built in recent decades and one which has the admirable title 'Stone Thing'. I also know a man who has just built himself a stone circle, presumably to dazzle future archaeologists.

World tourism, too, has resulted in the preservation or construction of imaginative buildings, whether they are in the trees, in ice, underground, underwater or the tiny pods of a Japanese bedroom; stimulation for tourism has become a driving force in eccentric buildings. In turn these buildings can themselves become enshrined, over-respected and then preserved and restricted, probably death for their future. I once designed an eccentric building which used much salvaged material, but which the current occupiers now believe to be an important, historic and ancient structure, thus proving that imagination and belief are often more important than fact.

Architecture has become a much more popular subject for study, but one that ignores the history of buildings and is over concerned with regulation and social or political theory, when the major element in any design should arise from relationships and need. Practicality should be more important than amazing design, a requirement all too often overlooked. The perfidious influence of regulation, which has in many ways destroyed the use of proportion in design, remains a personal bugbear, as does the endless committee work now associated with proposals for any building or its alteration.

It is incredible, but true, that in some areas, planning applications presented for approval are put before a gentleman called a *'Police Designing Out Crime Officer'*. This is a full time policeman whose responsibilities include approval of any planning application. Few novels can match reality.

This book started life as an examination of architecture and its interaction with social change and fashion, an overambitious and pompous target for a light hearted bit of rubbish. It was also intended that the drawings would form a logical historic sequence, starting with the arrival of the common cold and the warm cow, followed by the exile of the warm cow and the invention of the chimney. These proved difficult to draw, so the concept, and many other ideas and scurrilous notes, were, despite the good intentions, soon abandoned.

My daughter sent me the outline for a sketch which was also beyond my drawing ability. She described it as:

'A classic thatched cottage in the style of an Italian villa with an elegant extension inspired by a passing Indian requiring space for romantic reading. The chimney, 'which makes a statement', is sited 1.2 meters from the villa in accordance with regulations. The dwelling is built in the grounds of a medieval dog house'.

These pages are intended to amuse, and not, like most cartoons since the 18th century, to be destructive or derogatory. Criticism is always easy; it may be difficult to play an instrument, or dance ballet, but we can all claim to be a music or ballet critic and raise a smile by criticism and negative comment, yet be unable to dance or play a note.

The negative mother-in-law joke is laughed at world-wide, but an audience does not recognise, because it is not funny, that many mothers-in-law are decent human beings.

These pages are, instead, intended to be positive, even if the suggestion that the sky is blue and the fairies are skipping does not normally get you applause.

They may also be difficult to categorise. With an eye on royalties, I tried to work out how this book might be recorded in the libraries of the future, but was unable to decide whether it would be listed under education, history, architecture, blasphemy, life style advice or philosophy. I am going to plump for philosophy.

Comments on the modern world can often be overtaken by events. Such events can, themselves, be so extraordinary that the extraordinary seems ordinary. This is certainly my impression of the modern world and underlies the view behind these drawings.

I hope they may provide a moment's entertainment.

FASHIONS OF THE FUTURE
Helter Skelters and a Bus Shelter.

A study of history suggests that the politicians and events of our day will soon be forgotten. With the rising waters of global warming, cities will disappear, taking with them transport, trade, and, perhaps, politicians. The architecture of the future may be restricted to underground bunkers, grass covered eco-houses or derelict, squatter-inhabited city ruins. Even so, building design will continue to be defined by social trends, fashion and geography.

The illustration shows a design for inexpensive housing. The Helter Skelter house is a prefabricated unit, requiring no foundations. Styles may change, but not our memory for health and safety regulations, which will form an essential part of the oral tradition. The Helter Skelter therefore retains a fire escape which is not only decorative but responds to the needs of historic custom. Tribal elders will talk of helter skelters as common in every seaside hamlet before they were flooded by the rising waters.

The Helter Skelter house will be seen as a stunning example of an admired lost heritage.

Each Helter Skelter is a small dwelling, using little land, in a world where land is scarce. Such buildings will be capable of individual decoration, thus meeting the demands on architecture made by social climbing. Gathered in hill top clumps, they are also capable of nomadic use, should a move be necessary through unsettled times or problems with relatives.

On the hill beyond the houses can be seen a small building which had originally been intended as a shelter for the legal enjoyment of tobacco. Global warming and the subsequent collapse of societies and trade, when combined with a new rigour in social behaviour (which will outlaw, unless chaperoned, the meeting of young men with ladies), will ensure that the original purpose of the shelter is forgotten. Just as has happened to hill top sites before, this hill top will become a sacred hillside, a tribal gathering place centred on a shelter revered as a shrine to that forgotten deity 'H & S'.

DEMOCRATIC DEBATE REORDERED
Step Pyramids

There is astonishing variety in political debating chambers. They come in all shapes and sizes, often derived from whether that government is dictatorial, charismatic, committee based, for single or multiple parties or for coalition government. Spaces for government debates have existed for millennia and have always been used for meetings called to justify tax gathering, and to allow an incessant amount of talking.

Given recent difficulties in England, a new design could improve the political environment and the mental state of the nation. The proposed design is a combination of two ancient respected buildings, the amphitheatre and pyramid.

The amphitheatre has stone seats for the baying press, and plenty of room for the mistresses or toyboys of delegates and for secret police or those enforcing political correctness.

A section of the amphitheatre is also reserved for lawyers and political advisors, who are provided with only one megaphone between them, so that only one of them can speak at a time.

The pyramid itself is reserved for the delegates, who sit on the rising steps, but with a different party on each side of the monument. This separation reduces the physical violence seen in so many parliaments. It also ensures that each party can shout to its heart's content without being heard by anyone else.

The rising levels of the pyramid also control promotion within a party, since an ability to climb should ensure that leaders remain young, fit, mentally alert and able to fight their way up.

The pyramid will have no roof. This omission should shorten speeches and weed out delegates not fit enough to survive a damp and windy existence.

As was the custom in the democracies of ancient Greece, seating is on cold stone benches. An alternative would be to use misericord seats to keep people awake. A misericord, when raised, has a ledge on which to perch. The seat then collapses downward should the user fall asleep.

All seats face outwards away from the pyramid. Although this means that delegates cannot hear the debates, it allows them to spend time playing with their smart phones.

The chairman of the typical government was once a king or dictator. In England, the meeting chairman is known as the 'speaker', presumably because he is not meant to speak. He sits in a small roofless room at the top of the pyramid, a room which is without facilities, in the hope that these omissions will shorten sessions.

Below the amphitheatre, in the space traditionally reserved for lions, are the offices of the most important of staff, those who process the salaries and expenses of the delegates.

Left: The Megaphone   Right: The Misericord Seat

PIGEON TOWERS & WORMS
New Sources for Food

It was not so long ago that farms or gentry properties with sufficient land kept pigeons. They were an important food source, particularly during seasons when other food and game were not available. The food came not from eating the adult, but from the young chicks or squabs, and the pigeons also provided eggs and guano. Most farms in Cornwall had rows of pigeon holes either made in existing buildings or in specialist pigeon houses and towers. There had been rules about how many acres you had to have before you could keep pigeons but such rules had long since fallen into abeyance and farmsteads with plenty of pigeon holes are to be found everywhere.

Future food shortages will focus attention once more on the delights of pigeon pie and therefore on housing those birds for easy gathering in specialist towers. Such buildings will, as they once did, prove a competitive way of establishing social status. No doubt there will be prefabricated, carefully designed pigeon towers to be bought for every home of the future.

The pigeon tower on the opposite page is that at Harlyn House, near Padstow. Intended as both useful and ornamental, it is surrounded by walls full of pigeon holes and was probably built in the 18th century, in imitation of a Mediterranean pillar dovecot. Some 14 foot high and 5 foot 6 inches round, it has 60 holes in five rows. The design is believed unique in England.

Pigeons are not the only overlooked food source which should be considered for the future. I am told insects are full of protein and can be tasty. Seagulls and their young chicks were also eaten in earlier centuries, although writers of the time complained of the taste. Other forgotten foods include limpets which, like other now popular 'scavenged' foods, can be a good source of protein.

There are those who swear, since worms are the food of the future, that 'vermiculture' will make your fortune and that a cellar full of worms is a sensible investment. So there will be a fashion for a 'vermiculture house' or 'worm stable'; I look forward to seeing what these buildings look like.

The Worm Cookbook, (which I do not want for Christmas) has probably already been published, since, although you can eat worms raw, it is better to cook them first in case they have parasites.

Their food value is such that it seems all too likely that a dictator of the future will, when under pressure from a starving proletariat, cry: *"let them eat worms"*.

A FLYING VISIT
The Towers of Ireland
Glendalough, County Wicklow

Glendalough is not only one of the most beautiful of landscapes, but also the site of a monastic settlement founded in the 6th century. Such monastic settlements were hamlets which included a number of scattered houses and chapels, as well as communal buildings. At Glendalough they are loosely grouped round the home of the founding holy man, St Kevin.

The monastic buildings at Glendalough include one surviving isolated tower about 30m high. This is one of some 120 such towers which, with only one or two exceptions, are unique to Ireland.

Although the buildings of Glendalough were built of stone, with stone roofs, such towers were not often built on sound ground or good foundations. Instead the circular tower was strengthened at its base by having a solid fill above the ground. This in turn meant that since they were not hollow, their entry doors were up in the air.

It has never been certain why the towers were built to this design and their purpose remains a much debated subject. It had been suggested that the towers were intended as lookouts, as places of refuge, as store houses, or as buildings of display and status.

It is only now that we are able to explain the true reason for the building of these beautiful and famous towers. They were of course associated with the invention of woollen socks by monastic hermits, and their realisation that in the narrow marshy valleys of Ireland the monks were being overlooked by the flying sleigh of Father Christmas. The Celtic monastries therefore developed their tower so as to hang their socks high and remedy their Christmas isolation.

So it was that monastic socks, hanging high in the air so that they could be filled from his sleigh by a racing Santa, were the reason for the building of the magnificent slender towers of Ireland.

A TROJAN HORSE
The International Gift

The story of the Trojan Horse is of how the City of Troy was defeated in the 12th century BC, when the besieged inhabitants received the gift of a magnificent model horse. Unfortunately, in the horse were hidden soldiers who then opened the gates to the attacking Greeks., a story which is also the orgin of the phrase: *'Beware of Greeks bearing gifts'.*

A more realistic and cynical view of history suggests that there was never a Trojan Horse full of soldiers, but that the story arose from the Greek habit of giving affectionate names to their machines of war. Thus their greatest battering ram was known as 'Horse' and was used on Troy shortly after those walls had been weakened by an earthquake.

However, doubts about the story should not prevent us being alert to the dangers of the foreign gifts or inventive ideas used by people in one country who wish to get to another. We can assume that the rich or powerful will, as always, find a way to overcome bureaucratic problems at a border.

Alerted to this problem we need to look out for Trojan Horses gathering on the cliffs of France. These magnificent animals can be expected to have, hidden within their vitals, the bunks, executive lounges and hiding places of business men hoping to leave for a new life in England.

The candidates could include bankers, Russian oligarchs, and the 'Euro-Rich' who will soon realise the benefit of their commissioning an art work large enough to contain them and their entourage. We also need to look out for subtle Brussels bureaucrats who, realising the futility of living in the Euro Zone, wish to flee to Britain, but will first award themselves a 'Euro-grant' for a work of art which, intended for shipping to a trade fair in Britain, would be large enough in which to hide themselves and their families.

A more positive use of the Trojan Horse concept would be to use them to spread our influence and trade with other countries around the world. What could be better than to ship dozens of these horses as trade gifts 'from a friend'? We should perhaps exclude from the list Greece, and Turkey who might claim they had seen the horse before, and North Korea, who would probably blow it up.

Above all, our watchword should be caution and suspicion; we should beware of anyone bearing gifts and in particular, any unusual gatherings, particularly of horses, on the cliffs across the Channel.

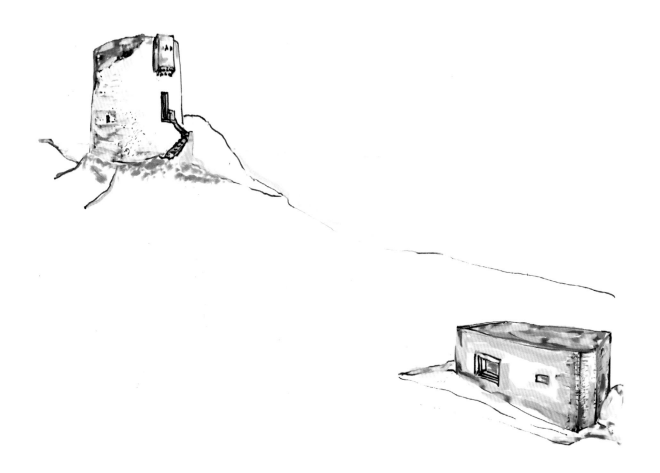

MARTELLO TOWERS & PILLBOXES
Nationalism and Migration

Britain is an island which has not been invaded for centuries. However, the sea has not prevented the country from devising many schemes for protection against invasion. These have included the great forts of the Normans, many arrangments of ditches and embankments, and the coastal gun forts of Henry VIII.

A Napoleonic era scheme required Martello towers. These, based on a 16th century tower in Corsica, were small forts first built after 1805. About 140 were built in Britain, most of them sited on the coast to guard against French invasion, with a further 50 odd built in Ireland. They were all about 40 foot high, had two floors and were garrisoned by an officer and 24 men. Designed to resist cannon fire with round towers and thick walls, their flat roof was a good site for a heavy gun, able to fire all round the horizon. They never had to resist the French but became useful to the Coastguard in their fight against smugglers. The invention of the rifled barrel made them of no further use. Some 47 Martello towers still survive in England today.

Another spate of tower and fort building against the French took place after 1860 when Palmerston was Prime Minister. Known as the *Palmerston Forts* or *Follies* they included the Palmerston forts in the Solent, criticized for facing the wrong way and outdated as soon as they were built.

Finally, faced with a real fear of German invasion in 1940, the country was laced with concrete pillboxes intended to hold up an invasion force.

Partially prefabricated and erected in a hurry from May 1940 onwards, they formed defensive lines guarding beach heads, roads and river crossings; an astonishing 28,000 were built in lines of defense that snaked across the country. There were six different designs for varying types of gun and site, but all the pillboxes were basic, cramped, cold and dark.

I know what they were like because I grew up with one in the garden. It was only seven years old when we moved in, having been built in 1940 to guard a river crossing of the Arun. Our pillbox was a type 24 and had a loopholed portico to cover the entrance and just one large gun embrasure for a 6lb gun. We used the pillbox for keeping geese, who seemed to me to be jolly dangerous.

This examination of the many defensive buildings around the coast and the survival of so many today, suggests that the towers could now provide bases from which to defend the boundaries of the country not against invasion, but as monitors of the coast and to control those wishing to flee the country.

In the political turmoil that is likely to embrace Europe and our neighbours for the foreseeable future, and in view of the endless debates on emigration, it seems wise to ensure that we should retain the wonderful people of Britain before they wander away. We are fortunate that the sea surrounds our coast, and that we already have in place a coastal defense or *population retention scheme*, the *PRS*, that can be of use in the future.

IGLOO CONFERENCES
Business in the North

Professional or trade conferences can be enjoyable. They often take place in exotic places where delegates will gain enriching experience, and learn how to balance fruit filled cocktails while looking seriously interested. It is unfortunate that such important gatherings are considered by the wives or partners of delegates to be dissolute orgies of dubious behaviour, of no benefit to the world.

Since global warming will soon make the Arctic a more desirable destination, it is therefore proposed that, as a change from the waving palms and naked bodies of the south seas, purpose built conference facilities in the north could ensure stern concentration and a reduction in the frivolity common at such events. The illustration gives an idea of the facilities available.

- Each delegate has his own igloo.
- Since, in order to meet international guidance on energy conservation, neither the bedrooms nor central conference chamber are heated, all delegates should bring warm clothing.
- No matter how long each session might last, relaxation will be possible in the bar where delegates may, while hunched over their drinks for warmth, review their lives with the barman. All drinks are served with a lump of ice. The design of this bar was based on parts of the Québec Ice Hotel, where visitors really do shiver with delight in an eccentric building of ice.
- For sport and exercise a lucky delegate can spend the day trying to catch fish through a hole in the ice. The hole is recut each day.
- Delegates attending a conference late in the year should bring stockings since Father Christmas starts his world tour with early stocking filling flights in the north.
- Please be aware that stockings are likely to freeze solid.

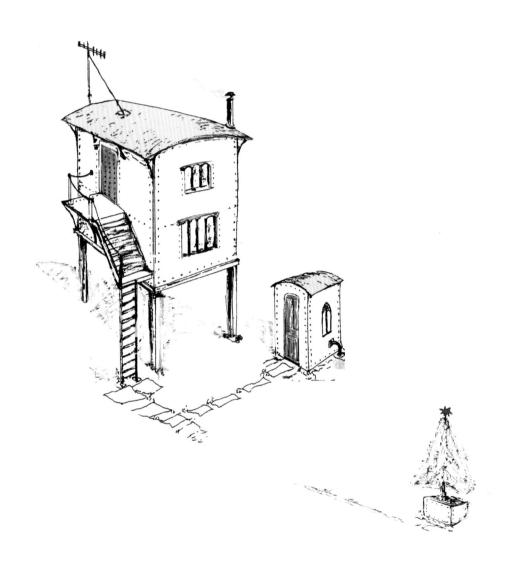

THE OLD WATER TANK
A Retirement Home with Sous-suite Facilities

The renovation and conversion of old buildings has been one of the enthusiasms of recent years. By now, there can be few farm barns still available for alteration and the pressure to find projects and to provide programmes for ever more desperate television hosts has resulted in the renovation of ever stranger buildings. Even this author once converted a small public lavatory into a desirable residence. The shortage of buildings for reuse has meant that the most unusual are now considered viable and 'imaginative' projects.

The illustration shows how a hill top water tank became the desirable retirement home of a city banker and bonus spender. Permission for alteration was allowed on the basis that the tank had, as part of essential services, formed part of a residence and therefore had residential status. This tasteful renovation, carried out in the dark years of a considerable housing shortage, was much admired. It is expected to be listed as a building of national importance.

In 2002, the improved building was entered in the prestigious award scheme of the local conservation society. The judges' attention was drawn to a skillful renovation, which included mullioned windows to the end gable and a Gothic window to the lavatory.

Rivets were retained as structural and decorative features and access was improved by a platform outside the front door, with attached rope guard rail. The use of a tricky lower section to the access ladder was explained as necessary to reduce visits by relatives.

Outside, the small sous-suite 'facilities' provide every modern convenience, and make unsightly pipes to the main tank unnecessary. This little building is a coherent and carefully co-ordinated extension which contributes to the architectural ensemble.

Sadly, the judges did not like the television aerial, which was thought an unnecessary addition to the skyline. Others of the panel were concerned that the lack of gutters would disconcert visitors, and contribute to the rusting of the structure. There was some discussion as to whether the black tarmac to the roof was an appropriate and sympathetic finish in a country landscape.

The judges also pointed out that the owner, who had studied at Hogwarts School, not only refused to allow the location of the Water Tank to be revealed, but insisted that he himself remained anonymous.

The entry did not receive the acclaim that its architect felt was due, particularly as it was not even shortlisted for the award.

HOLIDAY RETREAT
With Detached Closet and Settlement Pond

The Romans had praised the joys of the countryside but it was not until the 18th century that the English started building follies where it was intended that you should sit, admire the country and contemplate, rather than hunt, travel or fight. This was the age of a wealthy middle class who could live off investments, had time on their hands and could spend money in a relatively peaceful and settled land.

Follies and ornamental buildings of no particular purpose became desirable demonstrations of status. Gardens and parks were changed from the tightly constructed gardens of the previous century to 'romantic' landscapes demonstrating the owner's sensibility and awareness of nature, the value of a view and the owner's interest in the more unusual architecture of distant countries.

It may be that today's thriving business in holiday cottages has developed from that earlier interest in building follies in which you were meant to sit, rest and think or look.

In practice, I suspect that few people really want to just sit and contemplate. I once converted an earth closet by a lake as a place for visitors to sit, read and admire the scenery. It was never used.

Holiday cottages are visited 'for a break' and are often small places, beautifully fitted out, in which you find that you do not know what to do with yourself, where the possibility of family conflict increases, and from which you long to return home so as to write a letter complaining about the facilities.

The little building illustrated is set on a mound to provide a view over the countryside. It is a picnic pavilion for a day out, reached either on horse or on foot. Designed by a landowner with no special knowledge or interest in architectural detail, it was intended only to suggest the owner's learning, cultured travel and social status.

In recognition of the changing habits and standards required by visitors, the retreat has its own *'House of Convenience'*, which is set by a smelly settlement pond, itself an early example of ecological planning.

Typically, no provision seems to have been made for staff, servants and attendants.

A. Dung for Sale
B. Customs Service: Complete All Forms
C. World News: We Cover Disasters
D. Rescue & Lifeboat: Reserved for the Deserving
E. Immigration: Two Generations Proof Required
F. Secret Mission: We are just spying. What are you up to?
G. Health and Safety Executive: Working for You
H. Official Papparazzi

J. SAL: Society for Animal Life
K. Supplies & Needs Co: Everything for your Voyage
L. Go Green, Eco & Life Affirming!
M: The End is Nigh!
N: IBO: International Belief Operatives
P: Please can I have your Autograph?
Q: Social Services: Counselling & Support
R: Get out of my way! I'm racing!

The Ark has a raven and dove, both ready to go.

NOAH'S ARK
With Sea View and Accompanying Fleet

Noah saved his family and animal stock by building a boat, in a tale that is told by every culture and continent of the world. The study and history of floods and disaster is fascinating. A couple of examples emphasize the size and power of such disasters. Volcanic eruption and the subsequent tsunami destroyed Santorini, the Minoan civilisation and, perhaps, Atlantis. More recently, when Krakatoa erupted again in 1883, land vanished and its effects were felt for thousands of miles. It is said that its force was greater than many nuclear bombs.

More recently, the world has become certain that global warming will produce immense floods, that tsunamis will sweep inland and that our civilisation will be in trouble.

Since we should get a boat ready that can float us to safety, we should therefore study what made Noah's voyage a success.

The story of Noah's Ark is one of survival against the odds; even the word 'Ark' may have meant 'safety box' rather than describing the boat type. In consequence, there are as many theories as to what the boat looked like, as there are people who write on the subject.

Noah's boat was probably not the round bilged vessel imagined by medieval artists. It may have been a raft, or a square punt-style box boat, but was most likely of pitch covered papyrus reed, a design that fits with the use of boats in the ancient middle east. It was a reed boat that Thor Heyerdahl sailed across the Atlantic and another, the *Tigris*, that he sailed around the northern Indian Ocean. The description of the Ark in the Bible, which worried many a medieval theologian, could describe a raft or papyrus reed structure with a box-like superstructure.

Having decided that the Ark was a reed boat, and that therefore this was the design to be copied when preparing for a future flood, one also has to remember that, in this modern age, any such survival voyage would need a support fleet.

For instance, there is no room on the boat for the tall pigeon tower, the tree for ravens, the animals' varied and different food supplies, or the necessary number of life rafts, or the vital computer centre needed to record the animals. Sewage and dung disposal needs to be planned as does re-victualling and a host of other needs.

In reality, therefore, both we and Noah would be accompanied by a pretty large fleet. These boats will carry stores, dung, people from animal charities, from health and safety and from a host of other well-meaning bodies. They in turn would form an armada who would themselves need a further support fleet.

Whether we can manage the paperwork and stress of managing this fleet is open to doubt.

The drawing shows some of the support vessels necessary for successful survival from flood.

TREE PALACE
With Swing-and-drop Garderobe

The late 18th century saw a dramatic expansion in, and enthusiasm for, garden ornaments, follies, and buildings designed to set off the landscape, or to provide a focal point. Small pavilions also formed an objective for walks and rides. The follies of the late 18th century were intended to amuse. Such buildings included tree houses, which, despite some 18th century examples, were more numerous in the late 19th century.

The Victorian folly illustrated shows a miniature classical pavilion neatly set in a tree. The branches of the tree have been pruned and cultivated to provide the best support.

Such a house is not only the perfect children's play house, but was also probably a place for romantic assignation or for love affairs with gamekeepers. Of sufficient size to be a permanent dwelling, it is thought that eccentric Uncle Arthur lived here in the years before the first World War.

The 'necessary house' was detached, as was usual at the time, so here the facilities had to be built in an adjoining tree. The 'air' closet is easily reached by swinging across on a wooden-seated trapeze.

It is not known how this air closet was emptied. The suspicion exists that, as in many an ancient castle, this hut's air closet offered only 'drop' facilities.

However, the siting of the garderobe assures a certain measure of hygienic protection and reduces the foul smells which might otherwise ruin a perfect summers day.

For many gardeners, authors and artists of the late nineteenth century, the existence of fairies at the bottom of the garden was, like the wisdom of politicians, a deeply respected belief. The addition of two gnomes delivering a Christmas tree is therefore an appropriate example of the enthusiasms of the time.

The confusion illustrated by their cry *"Where shall we put it?"* is merely the traditional call used by the staff of every delivery service that has operated through the centuries, although in this case it is possible that the choice of trees may have caused genuine difficulty.

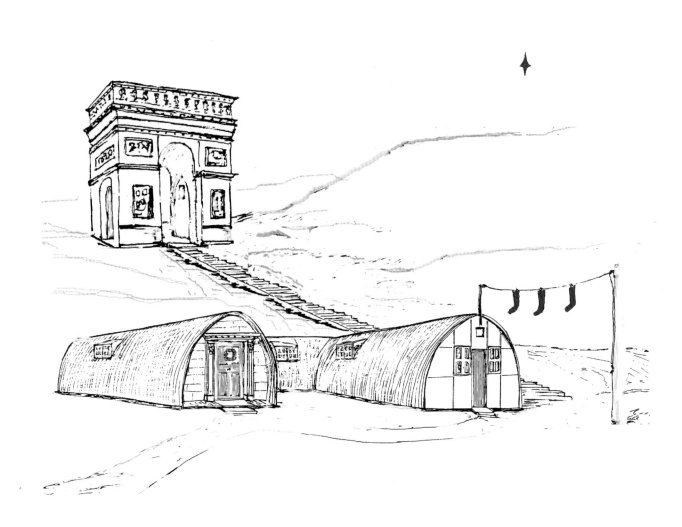

HISTORIC HOUSE
Bien Équipé de Toilette de Triomphe
Nissen Huts and the Arc de Triomphe

Corrugated iron has been used for buildings since the 1840's. It was once considered a great technological breakthrough, and corrugated sheets were exported everywhere.

The early importance of corrugated iron lay in its use for prefabricated units, which were exported to provide housing during the 19th century expansion of settlement and trade in Australia, America and any land where new settlement took place. This colonisation would not have been possible without such prefabricated packaged houses. At one time 45,000 such dwellings were being exported to Australia each year.

It is a shame that few examples of the grander buildings survive. Who would not wish to admire the sumptuous palace built in 1843 for King Eyambo of Calabar, first erected in Liverpool, so that visitors could see round the prefabricated structure? On arrival in Africa, it is said to have disappointed the client, since the noise of rain on the iron sheets deafened all those inside the building.

Corrugated iron is now remembered chiefly for Nissen huts and government encampments, but there are still many small iron churches, village halls, sheds, and farm buildings which the passage of time has rendered interesting. In Australia, some of them now have Heritage Building protection.

There is still time to consider preserving the few buildings that remain, usually as small village halls, garages or other utility buildings. A corrugated iron house is a rare sight since, unless well protected, the older buildings eventually rust out.

The round-roofed buildings associated with corrugated iron sheet were originally designed by Lt Col P N Nissen. The illustration shows a configuration common for such buildings, although this example has been personalised by the proud owner, who added an ersatz Georgian door surround to his otherwise standard building.

Believed to be an admirer of the French, he also built a splendid outside W.C. with fine views across the countryside. This splendid convenience is known as *The Triumph'* in honour of the larger version in Paris.

The owner liked to be reminded of his *triomphe* each time that he visited the building and would jubilantly ring the bell mounted on the roof to signal a successful conclusion to his visit. It is unfortunate that noise abatement regulations required the removal of the bell.

Although drainage systems should normally be down-hill from a dwelling, architectural imitators should note that, in considering the siting of 'The Triumph', the view from the 'facilities' was given precedence.

SPEAKERS' CORNER
The Architecture of an Improbable History

Around 1750, a Town Council decided to build a market cross to promote the importance of the town and improve the declaiming of civic announcements.

Funding was provided by an elderly councillor who claimed his mother tongue was not the pervasive common slang, but a more poetic patois which he hoped to revive. Erected in 1758, the monument therefore reflected the wishes of its principal financier for better public speaking and the retention of a 'true' language.

The architectural design combined classical elements with a Gothic revival spire. A covered area allowed speakers to shelter from inclement weather. Platforms with flanking pillars provided a demagogic base and reference to the oratory of ancient Greece. The spire contained a sculpture thought to be either the founding councillor, or Demosthenes, the orator. Although originally known as 'Speakers' Corner', it soon came to be known as just *Speakers*.

Sadly, the structure was considered the resort of madmen to whom no one listened, and the Council, sensing trouble, used it as a market store. *Speakers* then became a resort for courting couples, where four, even eight pairs could, at a pinch, canoodle in the romantic gloom of dusk. This use as a lovers' tryst has endured in the phrase: *'Do you want to go Speakers?'*.

However the seats were hard and cold and the resulting complaints by uncomfortable women are said by some wits to be why women in this town learnt to do all the talking.

Further changes were made following Samuel Gurney MP's new association to provide drinking fountains and troughs to eradicate cholera and intemperance. In 1865, his movement encouraged *The Ladies' Association of Gentlewomen for the Promotion of Cattle Troughs & Abstinence from Alcohol* (The LAGPCTAA) to pay for the fashionable troughs to be built near the cross. The classical pillars then became hitching posts. A saying of the time neatly combined the historic uses of the building: *'Only horses will listen to a politician'*.

Further changes occurred with the decline of horse traffic, the arrival of the motorcar, and an interest in clean streets and so in 1905, *Speakers* found new use as a public lavatory, a use that still fulfilled one of the founder's objectives since it remained a popular but clandestine meeting place.

Then came disaster when not only did legislation prevent the meetings at *Speakers*, said to take place between those of like minds, but such *rendezvous* also caused moral concern to the widows of the town. On a more practical level, it was impossible to provide facilities for the disabled in these converted lavatories.

The building was closed and did not survive the 20th century. After being boarded for some years, and despite the impassioned pleas of conservationists, a demolition order to remove the monument was slipped through a meeting of the Town Council, just after lunch.

Speaker's Corner is no more. The site is now used to provide parking spaces reserved for members of the Town Council.

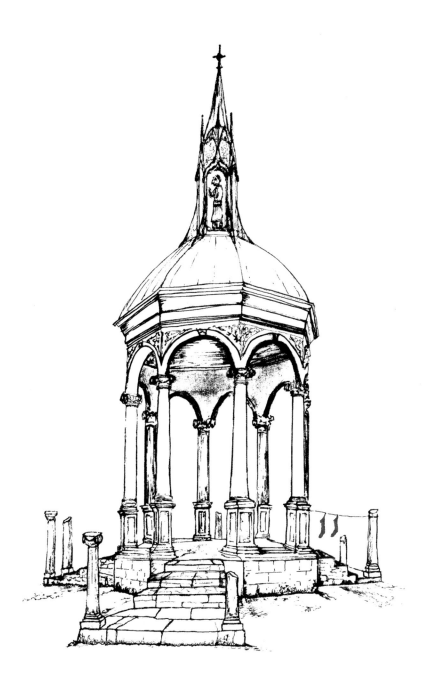

A: Chysauster B: The Cheesewring C: Fougou D: Lanyon Quoit: E: Men-an-tol: F: The Merry Maidens G: The Soil Pit

The drawing of the house is based on a reconstruction by English Heritage.

A CORNISH FAMILY HOUSE
Monuments of an Earlier Age

We sometimes forget that family life has been important throughout the history of man, and that buildings have been adapted to meet both his social and spiritual needs, but that the way a family works may not have changed much over the centuries.

Cornwall has many ancient monuments which reflect the history of an earlier civilisation. Some of these are shown in this drawing and include: Lanyon Quoit, Men-an-tol, The Cheesewring, Merry Maidens and Chysauster. The interpretations of their use is new.

Chysauster is a collection of eight houses, buildings and small enclosures, part of a once larger settlement in the far west of Cornwall. Thought to have been built around 200 B.C., each house has three or four rooms round a small courtyard, although there are new theories that one roof covered the whole. The round room was the main living space; the smaller round rooms and long room probably provided additional sleeping areas and space for storage, a water cistern and a cattle shed. Most of the buildings faced east, away from the south west wind.

The Cheesewring is a much admired natural phenomenon, which some have thought was erected for ritual purpose.

A Fougou may mean a cave, but is used in Cornwall to describe those *souterrains* associated with the culture of those who built hamlets like that at Chysauster. Fougous were in use from the late Iron Age to the end of the Roman occupation and were once relatively common. The one at Halliggye is 90ft long and has small offshoots difficult to crawl around. The purpose of these stone lined and roofed tunnels still remains uncertain. My own belief is that they were probably intended for early staging of the ritual 'Sardines'.

Lanyon Quoit, north west of Penzance, has a 17 foot capstone, replaced in 1824, and stands on 5 ft high supports. It was originally a chamber tomb or picnic-table.

Men-an-tol is also north west of Penzance and the main stone has a hole two foot across. Passage through the hole was long said to be a cure for pain and rickets, but its original purpose was, of course, not as a dinner gong, but as a post box for the daily stone tablet delivery.

The Merry Maidens is a set of 19 stones set in a circle within St Buryan Parish. The word 'maidens' is probably a corruption of the Cornish word for stone: *Maen.*

The soil pit is an early but common example of 'green' recycling.

Whether these often large monuments are natural phenomena or were manufactured for religious or other purposes is still debated. This drawing shows an interpretation of their original use which is therefore a new contribution to learned literature.

BLOWN BY THE WIND
Loughcrew, County Meath

Loughcrew was once the centre of an enormous estate in Ireland. The main house was burnt down three times before the owners gave up, and this portico is all that is left of the house that burnt in 1964. That house, designed in the short-lived Greek revival style by Charles Robert Cockerell, had been finished in 1829. All that now remains are the fine and varied service buildings. Of these the magnificent orangery and greenhouses have been renovated and converted to become the main house.

The distant walled gardens adjoin a church, or former tower house, called in honour of the improbably named 17th century Saint Oliver Plunkett.

In the hills above Loughcrew there are ancient mounds, passage tombs with stories of sun worship and of mythical ancient peoples.

Loughcrew is therefore one of those rare places where centuries, even millennia, of history and human settlement are on view in one place. As the wind blows over Loughcrew, the sentimental philosopher might consider of what little importance are the buildings of ambitious men, and how they will all fail. Renovation and imaginative architecture will come to nothing, but the hills will live for ever.

A more practical philosopher might suggest that, in view of the currrent outlook for the world, the sensible and wealthy man should build a large nuclear bunker deep below those hills.

I visited Loughcrew a few times and was always fascinated to find not only lots of life and activity there but also that the Irish lived up to the eccentric character often ascribed to them in novels.

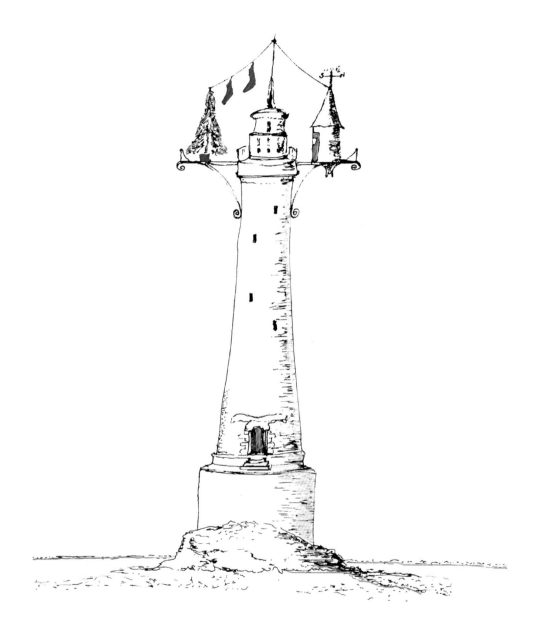

REDUNDANT LIGHTHOUSE
With Terrace and Sea View

Modern navigation systems and remotely operated lights have done away with the ancient trade of light house keeper, and hence done a great disservice to the crime novelist. Gone are the days when a howling gale could beat on the windows outside, while a lone watchman cowered inside before dying at the hands of a mysterious and unseen visitor, leaving only a cryptic note, written in his own blood, which reads *the crows... the crows...* There would also have been three cups of half drunk tea, and a small dog barking its head off on the floor below.

Like many once working buildings, lighthouses are now converted for other uses such as holidays. The difficulties of obtaining curved beds, tables and furniture are often overlooked. Many lighthouses are on dry land and have service blocks, but even those will be on a cliff, so that no former lighthouse should be visited by those with a fear of heights or who are unable to nip up a couple of hundred steps without getting giddy and out of breath.

Lighthouses are short of outside space and this illustration therefore provides the outside terrace required for gardening and for the Christmas tree, together with a counterbalanced platform for the facilities that a lighthouse with no septic tank cannot otherwise provide.

Many of the remote lighthouses were originally manned by teams who were changed regularly, but there are still many stories of how difficult it was for those who attended the lights to get on with each other, in so confined a space. A stay in one of these unusual buildings is therefore recommended either for those wanting to bring a relationship to an end or for those fleeing from their family or partners. Despite this, it is said that close confinement is often good for romance and so I suppose that a lighthouse holiday may provide many with an exceptional experience.

But if you are going to book a surprise holiday, make sure your partner has a head for heights, and that you only stay three days.

THE PAGODA WIND TURBINE
With Solar and Lunar Panels

It is regrettable that regulation, lack of imagination and political correctness discourage the building of follies or buildings of splendour. It is sad that so little effort and imagination is used to provide interesting or architecturally satisfactory designs for necessary but sometimes contentious buildings.

The drawing shows an award considered design for a wind turbine and prefaces a call for the redesign of all future turbines. In a more caring future, groups of turbines could include examples from different cultures such as a Hindu temple, or Turkish minaret. Why are wind turbines not designed to provide visual variety and architectural interest?

The wind turbine illustrated was designed as a multi-storeyed Chinese pagoda. But it does not depend just on the wind, since in addition to the blades necessary for wind power, the pagoda can also source both solar and lunar power from the panels fitted to the many roofs of the building.

Solar panels are fitted to the west, south and east on each of the 12 roof levels. This tower could therefore be installed with up to 72 generating panels, all of which should work at mid day.

Lunar panels, which are sickle shaped, are fitted in the remaining space on the 12 roof levels and they are intended to ensure power generation continues through the night.

So, even when the wind is not blowing, some of the panels will always face the light, and energy will be provided either by the wind or from the sun by day, or the moon by night.

But there is yet more we can do to improve our green credentials.

We are planning to make rainfall yet another energy source by collecting water at the top of the pagoda in an inverted funnel and tank. From this tank the water will run down across small paddle wheels on each pagoda roof. This will turn the water wheels which can then provide power, when the wind is not blowing, the sun is not shining and the moon is hidden by cloud.

A JACOBEAN TOURING VAN
With Status Ceiling and Luxury Appointments

Anyone who goes on holiday by car is familiar with the caravans used by so many as their beloved homes-on-your-back. However, there were not many touring caravans in the early 1600s and few went on holiday. In those days, all would walk or ride or, if incapable, lie in a horse litter or be dragged on a sloping stretcher behind the horse. Luggage went by packhorse and seldom by waggon. Most people walked, or if wealthy, rode astonishing distances.

Travelling in a carriage took a long time to become popular. An ineffective Act of 1601 attempted to discourage men from going in carriages, which was considered effeminate. In any case there were few roads suitable for wheeled carriages until the late 18th century, and in Cornwall wheeled traffic was almost unknown until then.

There is some difficulty in drawing a Jacobean holiday caravan. The vehicle would have been narrow, for narrow roads, and of waggon style with a strong ladder chassis and very large wheels. The body was hung on leather straps from posts, and the carriage drawn by oxen or perhaps a line of horses. Journeys over the shortest distances took days. The reclining lady traveller may have had a maid with her. The coachman probably walked alongside, and the luggage followed in a pack horse train. The husband rode separately.

In order to demonstrate wealth and status, it is likely that the carriage would have been of ostentatious splendour. In this example, the open side allows glimpses of a single rib decorated plaster ceiling, such decoration being the most admired of the time. It is not known whether the 17th century traveller believed in the importance of hanging dice in the rear of a vehicle. This is therefore an imagined vehicle.

The earliest surviving coach in Cornwall is in The Royal Institution of Cornwall. Known as *The Trewinnard Coach*, it had been bought by the Hawkins family who then lived at Trewinnard. It is thought to have been commissioned for use in London by the Spanish Ambassador in the last years of the 17th century, and to have been sold because the ambassador did not pay for it.

This is a splendid vehicle, but used, it is said, mainly by the old Hawkins dowager to impress her status on the population by making a show when she went a couple of miles to church on Sundays. This was a journey that required the coach to be drawn not by horse, but to be dragged through the mud by a full team of oxen. It must have been quite uncomfortable, since its suspension still relied on leather straps. Sitting on the small benches the traveller would have been swung, bumped and bucketed.

THE GATEHOUSE AT LANHYDROCK
The Comfort Stop

From the early 16th century onwards, gatehouses and tower porches became the best of status symbols. They were not intended for defense but to show the importance of the owner and of his fashionable decoration. There are many surviving examples of both gatehouses and tower porches.

Some had guest chambers built over the entrance, or used the upper room for a banquet course or for tenant meetings. The smaller gatehouses and those with a tower porch built on the house had a tiny chamber over the entrance. This room might have been to store a family's weapons, to have been a prayer or saint's room, a marriage cell, a 'mystic room', or a room that ensured protection from evil spirits. No one is certain. My childhood bedroom was in one such tiny 'overporch'.

One of the last such gatehouses to be built was at Lanhydrock, in Cornwall, which was not finished until 1651, and now belongs to the National Trust. The gatehouse is particularly splendid and, unusually, is built some way away from the first courtyard of the great house. The upper room may here have been a dining hall and viewing point from which the ladies could watch a hunt or specially funnelled killing grounds.

Heaven knows where the ladies went, if they were stuck upstairs and 'caught short'. The gatehouse may never have been a *comfort stop*, but could serve as a prototype for that *necessary house*, way-station, or service station where a lady's coach or car might stop.

I would love to see more magnificence in comfort stops or motorway services. Wouldn't it be wonderful to drive off a motorway through a great decorated and pinnacled gateway?

Competition between designers of motorway service stations could produce wonderfully eccentric places, just as was the case on the earliest of the French autoroutes. Some might say this would cost too much. But, since money needs to be spent to get interesting buildings, I am all for giving a knighthood to those funding imaginative service stations.

The Robartes family of Lanhydrock had made their money not directly from mining but from selling miners the materials they needed and then lending those miners money at exorbitant rates secured against their investments. The Robartes fortune remains a good example of the adage that you should: *Never dig for gold yourself, just sell shovels to those who do the digging.*

THE BANK OF ENGLAND
A Budget Rebuild in the Architecture of Faith

In looking cheerfully to the future, we must ignore the problems of the financial system but can consider the hitherto secret plans for the new Bank of England building.

The earlier fine building by Sir John Soane was vandalised by alterations in the 1930's and abandoned by politicians in the 21st Century. It is therefore surely time to consider a new Head Quarters for the Bank of England and to ensure that its design and architecture reflect the importance of the institution in the life of the country.

First, the replacement has of necessity to be designed to fill the space available, which turned out to be the last tiny fragment of land in the City of London which was not owned by foreign investors.

Borrowing respectability and an aura of stability and strength from its neighbours, the design has an imposing entrance.

The design also includes features which reflect two thousand years of church building. This will, it is hoped, add further respectability to an institution that has struggled in recent years. This architectural allusion may encourage the return of that lost reverence which visitors once adopted when making a visit to a bank.

Although now much reduced in influence, the Bank will continue to operate in hope from the new building, which was designed in the tradition of corporate architecture and appears appropriate for the head office of a mighty institution.

The new Bank building has ample space for all employees.

It is hoped that the Bank's future viability will not depend on receiving presents from Father Christmas.

This sketch was drawn following the financial crash of 2009.

DEATH WITH STYLE
The Mausoleum at Pentillie

Pentillie Castle stands high above the Tamar valley and is a magnificent and eccentric house built by Sir James Tillie at the end of the 17th century. On a second hill stands a tower, also built by Sir James as part of his carefully designed garden of towers, walled gardens, long drives and avenues. The tower was probably intended as a place to which to walk, and in which to study or to entertain.

Then in 1713, shortly before he died, Sir James wrote a codicil which made the tower his mausoleum, and in which, in a newly dug crypt, he was then buried, sitting upright in a chair-like coffin. His burial gave rise to centuries of rumour and stories, but recent excavation has shown that he was buried just as the papers of 1713 had suggested. His burial was unusual but then burial had become a much debated issue for the country, since there was no more space within graveyards. Sir James' mausoleum is thought to be the first mausoleum ever built outside a churchyard in England.

The tower itself is an early example of a tower built as a place of repose or study; Sir James had also built another at his great country house in Wiltshire. At Pentillie, you climb up the hill, admire the view then enter the tower to look through the bars of a gate at the life size statue of Sir James sitting in his Jacobean chair, right over the place where his body was interred.

At a time when the future seems uncertain, let us hope that garden ornaments, romantic views and buildings built for joy, picnics and barbecues will once more become possible. No matter how gloomy the political or financial outlook may be, we can always plan a wonderful building to give pleasure both in retirement and after our life time.

However, bureaucratic regulation makes building for pleasure difficult, so we lose the originality, drama, eccentricity and brilliance that has graced England over the last three or four hundred years.

One solution might be to re-introduce ancestor veneration or make eccentric buildings fashionable. Today's self-important politicians will soon be forgotten, but the reviled Members of Parliament could ensure a glory that would outlive their present contemptuous existence if they were to erect small eccentric monuments to themselves, as so many others have done in the past.

Hill top towers will always be admired for their walks or distant views and as places for delight and picnics; they could also provide refuge from the floods of global warming and a defensible retreat when public order breaks down.

Although I would support energy-providing incinerators in which to place politicians and bureaucrats, other building designs should be more practical. New buildings should show commitment to 'green' issues, to the carbon footprint, global warming and rising floodwaters. It is also probable that, if of unusual design and ecological benefit, such eccentric designs would probably gain planning permission through confusion for the planning inspectorate.

At least let us have a debate and encourage eccentricity in the buildings of the future.

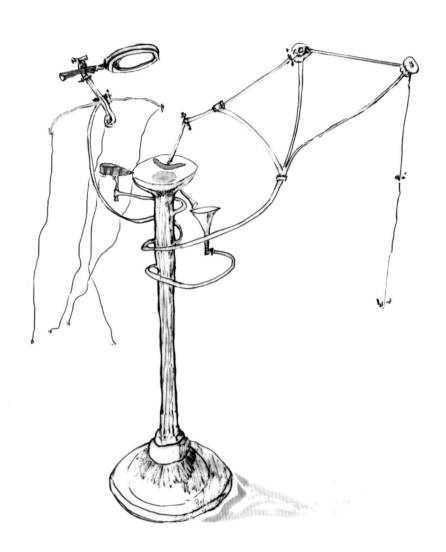

THE SOLAR SINGLE SAUSAGE SIZZLER
An Eco-friendly Barbecue.

Our friends continue to urge support for ecological issues. In response, we have designed *The Solar Single Sausage Sizzler*. This reduces the carbon footprint of barbecues and use of earth fuels to provide a truly 'green' cooking stove.

The barbecue is sited at the top of a high pillar, the better to attract the sun's rays, and is operated by a system of ropes and pulleys. A magnifying glass is mounted on a circular track and the glass is aligned with the moving sun so that it concentrates the sun's rays on and along the single sausage which is to be cooked and eaten.

Excess fat is collected through a funnel for ecologically satisfying reuse. Health and safety requirements are met by the provision of an almost automatic fire extinguisher.

The *'Sizzler'* therefore provides a method of cooking which ensures a material reduction in our carbon footprint.

Since only one sausage can be prepared at a time, there is additional benefit through a forceful decline in the over-eating that at present plagues developed nations.

Finally, the use of classical design elements is intended to fulfil the requirements of the most demanding planning officer.

Sadly, since patents are still pending, it seemed unwise to provide full details of the secret mechanism, so the illustration here is only an early concept sketch.

However. this brilliant idea has not been without its critics. My grandson says that cooking a meal would take too long and that this invention is 'rubbish'.

It therefore seems probable that the design for *The Solar Single Sausage Sizzler* may gather dust in this country and that it will remain yet another example of a great British invention which ends up being ignored in Britain until developed by other nations.

WELCOME TO BETHLEHEM
'The Town that's Better Known than You Think'

The Bethlehem Town Council commissioned this Nativity Card to promote their town and to provide a memento for visitors who would be coming to Bethlehem for the census.

Sadly, the drawing attracted a storm of protest and was condemned as inappropriate, politically incorrect, irreligious, blasphemous, and against the regulations not only of Health and Safety but of equal opportunity and equality of race and trade. The Bethlehem Committee for Public Contact and Ethnically Appropriate Tourism promptly withdrew the card, so that it has not seen the light of day until now. It is included here as an historic artefact, and as evidence of the illiberal cultural attitudes common when it was drawn.

The drawing combines several elements of the Christmas Story, including the stable, the shepherds, the three kings and Herod.

It also shows the flat topped adobe houses of Palestine, although many domestic dwellings of the time were more likely to have been nomadic structures rather than the mud brick buildings so often associated with the story of Christmas.

The drawing has its origins in an 1890 illustration of Bethlehem, although it seems likely that the famous inn and stable were further away, on the outskirts of the town.

A: Room at the Inn

B: Historic Structure: Bethlehem Council Historic Heritage

C: Herod's: The School that Cares for Infants.   All Welcome.
    Proprietor and staff are police approved and CPC checked.

D: Insert coin to see star: A Service provided by your Council

E: No Parking, Waiting or Loitering

F: Reserved for Three Kings: No Parking

G: Please Walk through Foot Dip.   Do Not Wash Socks Here

H: Health, Safety & Municipal Regulations
    applying to this building are lifted until further notice

J: 25 December: Designated Quiet Day
    No parties, singing, or disturbance of babies.
    By Order: Neighbourhood Watch

K: Shepherds: Please Leave Flocks in Enclosure.
    Form Orderly Queue.

L: Bethlehem Council welcomes you to this historic town:
    'The town that's better known than you think'

M: Antiques and Bric a Brac:
    New! Just In! Historic Manger Bits

N: Ye Olde Well

RISING WATERS
Re-use of the High Rise Block

Many of the world's cities started life as ports, so that climate change means they will be flooded and their skyscrapers left sticking out of the water. The Houses of Parliament will be reduced to a couple of short towers, Big Ben will chime in time with the waves, the dome of St Paul's will become a skating rink and Tower Bridge will become a danger to shipping. The unusual shapes and names of recent skyscrapers will ensure that the gherkin, pickle, cucumber and bunch of grapes will all look most peculiar when chopped in half and viewed from the sea.

Rising sea levels will put further pressure on the land available to live on, so that we now need to plan for sea-based dwellings, for reuse of half submerged skyscrapers and for the design of new sea-buildings to enable whole populations to live on the water.

Architects are already preparing wonderful but impractical plans which appear to make no provision for the reality of family or business life and ignore the shopping trip, getting to school and the need for sewers and rubbish collection.

My plans include converting the floors newly under water to fishtanks, adapting the floors which are level with the changing tide as sheltered marinas and, on the upper floors, leaving whole areas open to the elements, filling them with plants and also building green play areas cantilevered from the tower.

Every building will have several cranes, mooring slings, loading 'loggias', water distillation and sewage treatment plants, boat repair shops, taxi services and pick up points, helipads and enormous rubbish storage areas, in addition to hairdressers and massage parlours. One or two underwater floors will be converted to glamourous living space, live lobster hatcheries or training areas with underwater entrances for sub aqua enthusiasts.

For power, there would be a wind turbine and solar panels on the roof, together with both water wheels and the more powerful turbines powered by the force of the tide or stream.

Of course, it will all get out of hand. Planners are already proposing that *'designers will keep sustainability at the forefront of the project and aim to build a zero-energy urban structure to address both population density and eco-friendliness'*. I hope that my attempts at eco-friendliness will not land me in jail.

Such theorising does not deal with how drowned skyscrapers will rust, or how they will deal with tides, and the rush of flood water. Water and wind strengths may be comparable but their combined stength may shatter the towers and provide new plots for disaster movies.

Then there will be other problems such as social competition for a place in a sea block and arguments such as whether sea-dwellers must be able to swim and whether a landlord can claim wet clothes as tax deductible. And how will older residents get a newspaper delivery and find ice to put in their gin?

THE EXTENDED FAMILY
The Solution in Mud

The buildings of the northern half of the globe have seldom imitated designs from the southern half, and small house design has been restricted by the need to waterproof, by the ubiquitous concrete block, by tradition and by regulations.

South of the Sahara there are many exotic buildings and a similar variety exists on every continent, most of which reflect the human liking for decoration, status and the latest fashion.

Their smaller domestic dwellings use local materials such as bamboo, reed, wattle, or bent timber; a large number use earth or adobe and many roofs provide waterproof shelter during tropical storms. Although some have flat roofs, many are round huts with conical tops, whether built as a single-family hut, a cabin or as huts combined into a multi-cell house. They include impressive terraces, fortified homes, palaces and, at Djenne, the largest mud building in the world. The eccentric variety of buildings includes the reed huts and long roofs of Indonesia, the extraordinary decoration in Burkina Faso, Batak houses, snake-free raised 'basket houses', the timber and hay hut houses of the Chilean Mapuche ruca and the adobe villages of Mexico.

In Africa each culture has its own tradition in construction and decoration. Several countries stand out, but Sudan, Ethiopia, Mali, Basotho, Cameroon, Niger, Nigeria, Togo, Benin, Ghana, and Burkina Faso, Morocco and South Africa all have domestic buildings of varied, ingenious design and reflect the human drive to be different from their neighbours.

This drawing may give housing estate builders some practical designs for families and occupiers each of whom wants their 'own space'. Estate houses all too often lack proportion, common sense and space and are built only to meet the diktats of a building inspector. Houses could be designed to reflect other cultures and provide variety and invention instead of the usual small estate box. A new sense of proportion and practicality could, for instance, include wider and taller doors for the bigger people we have become. The 4ft wide door used in previous centuries would be practical and assist the disabled. Why can we not recognise that humans are changing shape? Why do housing estate vendors miniaturise furniture so rooms appear larger? Why cannot cheaper housing be designed to reflect our changed society and the way we spend time, which is of course often alone, crouched over a machine.

The illustration shows a tiny sample of delightful house designs, although not the variety of stone, moulded or painted decoration, and not the corrugated sheet shanty town buildings now common in all developing countries.

I prefer the complex mud buildings found in the family compounds of Kano, Nigeria, which allow for variety in family relations, privacy and togetherness and provide a flexibility that is perfect for the modern westerner.

And it is so easy to add another room for a guest, a relative, a mother-in-law or, if that is your practice, another wife.

Sidama bamboo, Ethiopia

Benin

Toposa Tukel, Sudan

Corbelled Karoo House, S.A

Cameroon

Ghana

Harran House, Turkey

Indonesia

A group of Trulli in an imagined hamlet

THE TRULLI HOUSES OF ITALY
Modular Houses and Family Life

These extraordinary Italian houses are now a charming tourist attraction. Trulli are found in the limestone heel of Italy where water, which seeps away through the rock, is a precious resource. So, farmers and smallholders dug out a cistern and over that they built round huts which were used as agricultural shelters and dwellings.

The houses are built with mortarless walls of small stones, which vary in thickness between three and ten feet. Built into the walls are children's arched sleeping alcoves, storage niches, and a fireplace and chimney, with, in the roof, a vent for air circulation. They are beautifully constructed with two stone skins, the inner of which is corbelled to form the dome. An independent outer skin has the stones sloped slightly to throw rain off the building.

The huts are usually in groups of 2 to 5, or, on larger farms, up to 12, so as to provide 12 spaces for one family. Many clusters include smaller rectangular Trulli for storage.

These beautifully constructed buildings were owned with pride and, as in any other culture, were personalised by elaborate sandstone carved pinnacles and decoration on painted roofs, with large, often religious, symbols.

Circular huts were the norm for the earliest dwellings and remained so for many cultures throughout the Iron Age. The late Iron Age culture at Chysauster gathered circular huts into one walled family unit. Such dwellings continue to be built by different races and cultures all over the world. Although it is not certain for how many centuries the Trulli have existed, it is not too fanciful to suggest that they too could be survivals of an ancient tradition.

A circular hut is of course cheaper to build than a building of square corners with quoins. The roof is simpler, stronger and there is no need for a mason to cut square wall stones. In 17th century England, the more cheaply built stone houses had rounded corners, and sometimes rounded chimneys, because this required less skill. It may also be that drystone walling is not dissimilar to stone hedge building.

I have always liked the idea that a dwelling could be a cluster of pods in a walled enclosure and do not see why the unimaginative house builders of Britain could not bring variety and interest to housing estates by producing an inexpensive prefabricated Trullo unit as the building block for houses of various sizes. This would also provide a market opportunity for circular furniture.

Such a modular house on one floor would have plenty of space for wives, relatives, children and dysfunctional families. In circular houses, you can sweep round corners and there is nowhere for burglars to hide. The complexity of a pod house plan would also give new life to the writers of detective stories.

THE HANGING GARDENS OF BABYLON
And the Lions' Den

Gardens remain an important part of a building's design, although it was many centuries before they were viewed as more than an enclosed space or social area. Today, gardens are all too often an ideal, a concept of pleasure, a working obligation rather than one providing genuine relaxation.

Among the earliest of gardens were those at Babylon, famous for its *hanging gardens* and, of course, for its lions' den. These gardens were an expression of status and of the exhibition through 'water features' of that rare commodity, water. I think that the closeness of the dens to the terraces discouraged the gardeners. In the end, there were so many fatalities in the dens, despite the good work done by Daniel, that Health and Safety officials discouraged gardening. So it was that a combination of death and bureaucracy brought to an end one of the seven wonders of the ancient world.

There is, however, one tradition which has survived the end of the Babylonian Empire, and that derives from the socks or *'Sok-os'* worn by the lions' victims. The socks were hung on the wall to record the daily feed and so were seen as a 'free present' associated with the lions' meal. This hanging up of Babylonian socks has evolved into the British tradition for giving Christmas presents, wrapped in socks, to be opened very early before breakfast.

After the loss of the hanging gardens of Babylon, tyrants appear to have lost interest in gardens. Other early gardens included those at the Sphinx and Pyramids, now identified, like the terraced pyramids of the Americas, as terraced gardens. Sadly, the Egyptians had overlooked the need for a lush climate that encourages plant growth. In Egypt, the sun dried terraces were therefore abandoned and garden ornaments such as the Sphinx, a forerunner of the ever popular garden gnome, became covered with drifting sand.

Stonehenge has only recently been identified as a showground for competitive floral displays. Organised by the Druids, the show's outer ring provided stands for exhibitors. The inner monoliths were reserved for the sacred mistletoe grown by the Druids. Cut and prepared on the so-called altar stone, it was sold to those attending the winter solstice, achieving great profits for the Druids.

The ceremonial greetings that accompanied the purchase of mistletoe developed the tradition that kissing can only take place under a piece of mistletoe. Sociologists have suggested that difficulty in sourcing mistletoe is the reason that many modern couples now marry so late in life.

Other little known gardens were in Norman Castles, the homes of owners with two obsessions, gardening and defence. This combination meant that only mushrooms could be grown within the dark walls. The mushrooms were therefore *'kept'* inside great towers whose floors were layered with fungi. This in turn gave the houses of the Normans the name, *'Keep'* by which they are now remembered.

A final example of historic gardening lies with the Eskimos. Unfortunately, the hours spent researching the gardening habits of Eskimos have been to no avail. I can only suppose that an Eskimo's gardening takes place in secret window boxes hidden within the igloo.

Research into the history of gardens continues.

THE PERFECT BED AND BREAKFAST
The Leaning Tower

Bed & Breakfast establishments have been around for centuries. Not only does my wife enjoy running a B&B at our home, but my work has included not just renovation of country houses but help in setting up new B&B businesses. Although my clients were unwilling to accept all the suggestions for improvement which are shown here, this experience has given me an unique insight into the operation of such a business.

The following pages illustrate the facilites to be considered for every B&B.

Reception and Welcome

The Leaning Tower was erected with European funding by the Historic and Tourism Amenities sub-committee of the local Council, the proposal having been approved at a time when a majority of councillors were on holiday. The project was intended to emulate the great Tower in Pisa, where visitors are in their thousands, usually following guides with multicoloured umbrellas. It was believed that the tower would attract visitors.

When it was finished it turned out to have a number of problems. The mayor refused to go to the top to declare the tower open. Health and Safety officers refused to allow public entry. And then, of course, there was a dispute with the building contractors, who claimed that the leaning tower was built exactly as specified by the delegated sub-committee.

After lying empty for some years, the Town Council eventually sold the building for re-erection at the B&B. In its new position, the tower provides good visibility of, and hence security for, the site. The tower also ensures that the home is easily identified by those without sat-nav. Despite its lean, it provides a useful office and linen store for the Bed and Breakfast although the owners are fed up with visitors who say: *'Take care it doesn't fall on you'* or *'Don't jump off'*.

Now that it is rumoured that the United Kingdom is leaving the European Union, the Council are concerned that the EU will want their money back.

THE OWNER'S FLAT
Preparing for the Worst: a House on Stilts

We worry about a doomed future for the world and live in gloom. Recent reports told us a tsunami would rush up the English Channel to drown us, or that global warming would melt the Arctic, raise sea levels, flood low lying land and so destroy our civilisation and way of life

Such concerns are not new. Not only have there been many real floods through the millennia but also many examples of unfulfilled warnings. In 1524 astrologers predicted the world would end with a flood, so that 20,000 inhabitants left London for high ground. In 1954, Dorothy Martin forecast a flooding and destruction of the world which never happened.

It was because of concern about rising waters that this Gothic Tower was built on stilts to ensure that the house would sit above future water levels. An additional benefit was that, as with some African or Indonesian homes, the stilts provide protection against snakes.

The secret of modern living is to try and find a helpful grant: the finance of the Gothic Tower is a good example of the benefits of research into little known grants. Such research got the Gothic Tower, first, a flood protection grant which, as it was built on stilts and on a hill, met the scheme's requirements.

Then a second grant was received towards its use for tourism and towards the site's B&B facilities. A third grant was obtained for the preservation of snakes and the costs of building a Serpentarium between the stilts. There is hope of a fourth grant being available for research into the use of snake milk.

Rising above the future floods, this high status, stylish building is intended for the owner's use, but is sited some way from the guest rooms, since it is widely recognised that no B&B husband likes to meet his guests.

The house has been judged a sensible design in a time of global warming, which will cause sea levels to rise, marsh and inland plains to flood and houses to be built in the air.

Fortunately, I am not worried about rising water levels, since I note that, in the spirit of *'I'm all right Jack'*, our own house is 300 foot above sea level. Even a tsunami coming up the Channel should leave us alone.

Yet more fortunate is our realisation that if there is a dramatic rise in sea levels and our house finds itself with sea views and right on the coast rather than four miles inland, we will surely benefit from an immediate increase in the property value of our house.

The drawing is based on 'The Field of the Cloth of Gold', painted c.1545, at Hampton Court Palace .

STONEHENGE & THE CLOTH OF GOLD
Parking and Breakfast

The Car Park

Stone Circles are found throughout Britain. Although often associated with rituals of the living and dead, there are many other theories for their construction.

All such theories overlook the obvious answer that any event of celebration would have required parking close to the ceremony. Stone Circles were obviously designed to provide that parking. These circular henges therefore offered spiritual protection for the transport used by the priests, officers and chieftains who presided at the gatherings.

It is appropriate that a Stone Circle should provide ordered parking for the perfect Bed and Breakfast. Visitors are asked to park neatly between the monoliths which are decorated with Christmas tree, holly and misletoe. You don't have to kiss anyone who you might meet under the mistletoe.

The Breakfast Room

The breakfast room remains the dramatic finale of many B&B stays. The illustration shows the ideal dining room, which is modelled on the 10,000m^2 palace built in 1520 by Wolsey for the young Henry Vlll of England at the Field of the Cloth of Gold, near Guines, in Northern France, where an astonishing temporary town was built for diplomatic meetings with Francis 1 of France.

Henry's great hall was an astounding piece of set-making with four wings, each thirty foot high, built round a courtyard. Part prefabricated, it had an eight foot high brick base below a timber frame with painted canvas disguised as stonework. It was heavily decorated with statues and plasterwork.

Such a breakfast pavilion should inspire wonder at breakfast and prevent comment by visitors on the quality of the egg and bacon.

TIME TESTED FACILITIES
A Guest's Needs

In planning to use or convert houses and outbuildings for the use of visitors, tourists, holiday makers or B&B guests, there are many facilities which must be considered. Solutions to some of these are suggested here.

First, security for prized possessions remains of concern for all travellers. A fougou recognises that a 3000 year tradition in stone lined and roofed passages or chambers can ensure that personal goods may be safe from the casual digging burglar. Access on hands and knees via the traditional creep ensures that deposit and retrieval are matters not to be taken lightly.

Second, it seems that bathroom and washing facilities are often thought important so the classic bath house **illustrated here** has a private plunge pool. Sadly, due to carbon restrictions, no hypocaust was possible and both bath and water therefore remain cold. This will be invigorating for visitors.

Third, there is often confusion in the use of the terms water and earth closet. It is the earth closet which has much to offer an Eco fanatic. The illustration shows a restored earth closet at my home which retains the slate covered side store for earth and effluent, a store which should be dug out at least once a month. The delightful brick house has just one luxurious wooden seat, assuring visitors of comfort and a fine view through the open door.

Finally, although pets are not normally allowed, some provision must be made for transport animals. A manger of classic Cornish granite is therefore provided for feed, and as a resting place for the occasional visitor unable to find room at the inn.

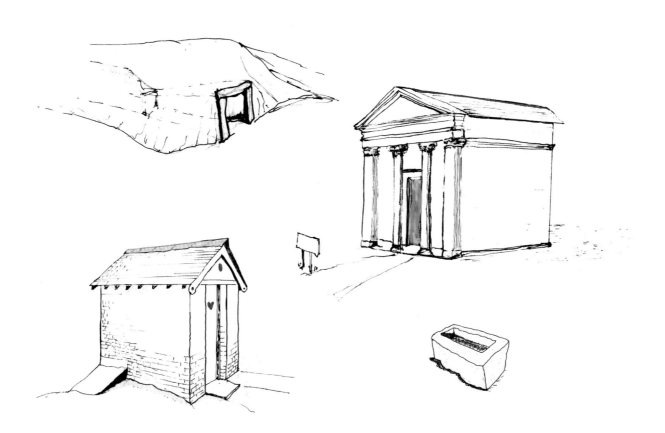

BEDROOMS
Five Suggestions for a Good Night

Bedrooms of varying price, style and taste are vital for the success of a B&B.

1. The reuse of sustainable materials is demonstrated by a tree house, which provides good sized family rooms for the adventurous.

2. To deal with concerns about rising water, a small boat has been anchored on high ground. Suitable only for two, it should allow visitors to sleep safely despite floods.

3. For those older visitors who require a malleable mattress, a hammock is the perfect answer. Separation of twin hammocks between different trees deals with marital snoring.

4. An eco-dome is the current enthusiasm of many tourists. This igloo-like bedroom provides minimalist protection, with efficient use of heat. An additional removable insulation cover ensures warmth in winter.

5. A luxurious bedroom is provided by the Chinese guest house. This provides drama, glamour and privacy. Beds are thin recyclable willow mats laid directly on the floor, and are said to be beneficial for those with bad backs

6. Despite considerable pressure to include Yurts and other uncomfortable tent-like rooms, these have been rejected as entirely inappropriate for a class operation.

PROTECTION & BELIEF
The Witch's Stone

We are lucky to have electricity to light the night. A power cut reminds us how frightening is the darkness and its noises. It is easy to understand that dread of night and the fear of spirits, ghosts and nocturnal creatures which terrifed earlier lightless generations. Following the Reformation in Europe, and the English abolition of the Catholic Church and their protective saints, there was an increased belief in superstition, witches and unseen dangers. The fear reached such extremes that there was an Act against witchcraft in 1563 and in 1597 James VI of Scotland wrote and published a book, 'Daemonologie', on the danger of witches.

A practical result of these fears was that there was a long period when, to ward off evil, buildings were built or fitted with items such as burn marks on wood or shoes hidden in a chimney.

One of the less well known of these defensive charms was a **Witch's Stone**. These are horizontal stones of some size which project from a building and are two or three foot off the ground and were built on outside walls to prevent the flight of witches. As a witch whizzes round a building on her broomstick, she would surely trip over the stone, crash to the ground and vanish, leaving the occupants undisturbed.

Most recorded examples date from the 17th century and are on outhouses rather than on the house although this is probably because the dwellings themselves have been altered and so the stones lost.

The picture not only illustrates a typical witch's stone but shows one still in place today.

Some years ago I was talking to a chief planning officer about the prevalence of 17th century Witches' Stones, only to find, some weeks later, that a planning permission sent to me included in its draft conditions the requirement that the *"building of a witching stone shall be submitted to and approved by the local planning authority. If the witching stone is ever subsequently removed by human agency or otherwise it shall be replaced ...before cock shut next ensuing after the time of its removal'*. I was about to question at what hour was cockshut and whether cockshut varied with the seasons, when I realised my leg was being pulled.

Nevertheless, the inclusion of a Witch's Stone could benefit many buildings. Their use would of course need to be in accordance with building regulations and more information would be necessary about the average height and weight of a witch, on whether modern diet had made a witch heavier than in earlier years, and on whether they still used the same flight path. Would the Stones have to project all the way up tower blocks? Could they not only ward off witches but also their modern equivalent such as solicitors or politicians?

Fears, worries and attempts to improve the home will never cease. Every generation has a different approach to the same issue, the defence of the home. This might be a Witch's Stone, or the *'little metal bottle tops, nailed upside down to the floor'* beloved by Flanders and Swan, or a fluid Feng Shui arrangement intended to harmonise your home.

Whatever the theory, it is clear that human activities, beliefs and concerns do not change much through the centuries.

ICE HOUSES
Protect the Ozone: Bring back the Yakhchal!

When I was a child *ozone* was a bracing mixture of salt, wind and seaweed, for which you went to the seaside. Sadly, scientists say that the smell comes from a sulphide gas. Now, the word *ozone* is used only to refer to the layer that encircles the earth and saves us from the sun's rays. This layer is apparently being holed and getting thinner from the activities of man; the damage is threatening the future of the world. Among the processes which damage the ozone and imperil the human race are the carbons, known as CFCs, used in refrigerators.

It cannot therefore be long before 'fridges are banned and we have to use natural ice.

Trade in ice was commonplace until a century ago. In Persia, a 3000-year-old system had 20 metre high pyramids called *Yakhchal* erected over cellars. In the winter, water, either transported from the mountains or brought in canals protected by walls, would descend to the cellar, freeze and then be kept through the summer. The *Yakhchal* was an astonishing engineering achievement, which could be copied today.

In 18th century England, ice was chiefly a fashionable aid to luxurious eating. Many gentry houses had a half sunk and domed structure known as the Ice House, some with imaginative folly style designs. Ice was also used for commercial purposes, but this was slower to take off. The ice store recently discovered under Regent's Park is a beautifully made egg shaped brick vault 9.5 metres deep, probably built around 1780 for domestic not commercial use.

The transport of ice from frozen rivers and shallow lakes to users in hotter climes has long existed. During cold winters, large blocks of ice were cut from frozen shallow ponds and freshwater lakes and then moved by waggon, or tramway to sale or store. The business was particularly well developed in the United States where 90,000 people were employed in a world wide trade by the late 19th century. Norway, another world trader, was exporting one million tons of ice a year. Improvements in refrigeration ensured that the trade in ice and ice harvesting came to an end during the early 20th century.

The illustration shows that a canal feeds both the *Yakhchal* and some shallow trenches, where water will freeze, before the ice is cut in workshops for storage.

I assume that, like the early toll houses, offices for the sale of ice could be designed to be interesting. This one has a rounded roof and windows that spell out the word 'Ice'.

Britain needs a new role in the world and ice trade under the motto *'Cut in winter and sell in summer'* could transform the country, so let's give it a go and not worry about what tariffs the WTO might apply to frozen water.

The 19th century ice tools include a cutting axe, small spitter, saw and both man sized and smaller block grippers.

RENOVATION & RECOLLECTION
Boconnoc, Cornwall

I have a long list of favourite country houses, but Boconnoc is at the top of that list. To arrive there after driving through its parkland landscape always raises my spirits. Boconnoc has only recently been resurrected after being empty and abandoned for many decades. Its condition had become so bad that its future was thought hopeless, many believing the house past repair. The house was listed among the top ten endangered buildings in the country.

Today, the house is not only in good shape, but remains the centre of an historic estate. It is no longer just an ancient decaying mansion but also a home and an essential contributor to the activities which ensure a future for both house and estate. The fifteen years of repair, funding and careful restoration were recognized by a number of awards including one for the best country house renovation in Britain that year.

Along the way the discoveries have included the dendro-dating of a c.1495 arch braced roof, the amazing, previously overlooked 18th century wall paintings to the great stair, and the carved remnants of the 1550 Great Gatehouse.

The work here provided a lifetime of experience and enjoyment, but, above all, that period recalls the friendship enjoyed with the owner who fought to rescue the house. Sadly, this great friend died shortly after the completion of the works. He will be remembered not only for his friendship, but also for the fun we had ensuring that the house was in sufficient condition to last a few more generations.

Boconnoc is one successful restoration, but it is not certain there is a future for this type of house or its devoted renovation. Is there the will power, the funds or the tax and financial system to support or even permit such a renovation in the future? Will such great houses continue to be seen as assets to a country or as white elephants not appropriate for a world which has moved on to other enthusiasms and interests? Will the supporting estate or other businesses that are necessary to the future of almost any large or historic house continue to be possible in a world of changing finance and tax or social and political theory?

Enthusiasms and interests go in cycles. Just as there was little enthusiasm for large and expensive old houses during the thirty years following the second World War, so the fashion for renovation and conservation of buildings appears to be coming to an end.

PUBLIC LAVATORIES
Essential Planning for the Future

Not many people worry about the sewers which take foul water down to lower levels for treatment, but which could be ruined by a flood.

Today, the papers are full of concerns about rising water and flooding, but since effluent is an unpopular topic, the flooding of our sewage system gets little discussion. A second more noticeable problem is the absence of public lavatories. Earlier ages found benefactors who built and donated splendid buildings for local benefit. Councils and Parishes also provided facilities which gradually became the only ones readily available.

Sadly, public lavatories are now a thing of the past. Not only have some become unsavoury meeting places, but they are often dirty and are difficult and expensive for a Council to clean and maintain. So the Councils have been shutting them.

We do not want to return to the habits of an earlier age, of which we are reminded by the notice *'Défense de Pisser'* painted in enormous letters on a wall in the High Street of Sarlat in France. Unless a popular movement claims that the use of public lavatories is a civil right requiring government funding, then we must try and find a solution that could provide Councils with an income-producing lavatory facility and, at the same time, solve the flood risk to sewers.

Since the main risk to a sewage system is flooding, lavatories should therefore be built at the top of a hill and sewage treatment carried out in reed beds on high ground. Reed beds provide natural cleaning of effluent and, by percolation through desiccated rock or gravel beds, the residue is clean when it joins the river system.

The proposal is for a tower of lavatory pods to be built on a hill. Since the pods would have wonderful views and luxury facilities, and could be easily controlled by a caretaker, since more could be charged for the higher level pods and since a franchised health, beauty and education facility could be at penthouse level, such a tower should generate enough money to fund maintenance. Building a tower of pods would provide plenty of WC units on one site. The high ground would reduce the risk of flooding; the carefully placed reed beds and ponds would deal with the effluent; the windy hill would reduce unpleasant smells near population centres and the numerous individual WC pods would remove the need to allow separate facilities for each of the increasing number of sexes now available to the human race.

The only downside is that the pods will be so nice that each pod will have to be automatically power showered to stop people moving in.

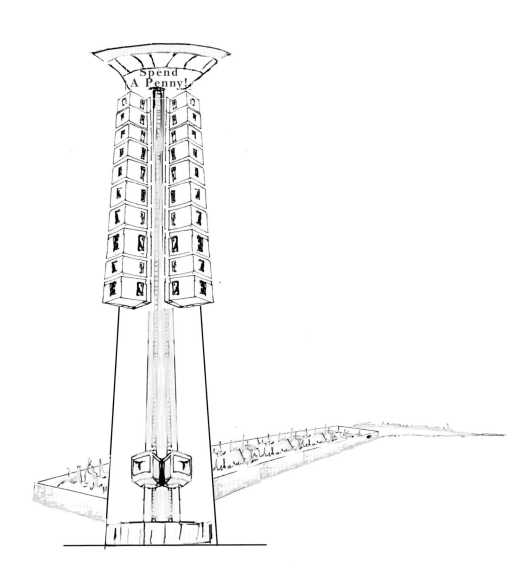

The red telephone box designed by Sir Giles Gilbert Scott, was based on the mausoleum of Sir John Soane.
Redundant boxes are now used as coffee houses, libraries, garden ornaments, shower rooms and for anything
except communication.

THE END OF COMMUNICATION
Messages and the Cleft Stick

When I was young, I wrote to family and friends using a pen with a steel nib. Nowadays there are few who use 'joined up writing' since most people use two thumbs to twiddle on a tiny palm computer for which there are no instructions. ("You can find out how to use this product at www....."). The makers of such tiny machines assume you have a degree not only in computer science but also in the new languages of machines, communication and 'social media'.

Throughout history, older generations have complained that *'It was nothing like this in my day'* and that all changes *'will certainly be for the worse'*. I understand this. I have always had sympathy for the man who could not cope with the invention of the motor car and so filled his car with water, because that is what a horse would have liked.

The changes that have taken place in conversation, social contact and communication are like a strange new automobile. Language has altered, conversation is reduced to odd grunts, communication is by a quick look at a screen and an unknown shorthand language. There is no use of pen and ink and I wonder whether I am from an extinct and forgotten race.

Some years since, we used to post hundreds of Christmas cards, since this was how we retained contact with those far away. Now we send just a few, partly because a more expensive postal service has been replaced by tools and networks with which I am not familiar, such as Twitter, Facebook, Blog, WhatsApp or other condensed acronyms, which probably include 'Grunt'. Keeping in touch is now done by making short hand notes on the machinery.

Changing fashion, different methods of communication and advancing years therefore suggest that we should celebrate the passing of the post box. It will not be long before the post box joins the telephone box, telephone, mobile phone, typewriter, fax machine and yodelling as a mystery of history. All have been replaced with inventions by science fiction enthusiasts.

Only the cleft stick may yet make a comeback. We must be positive and remember that reality can outshine the most extraordinary and apparently ridiculous prophecies.

A Cleft Stick

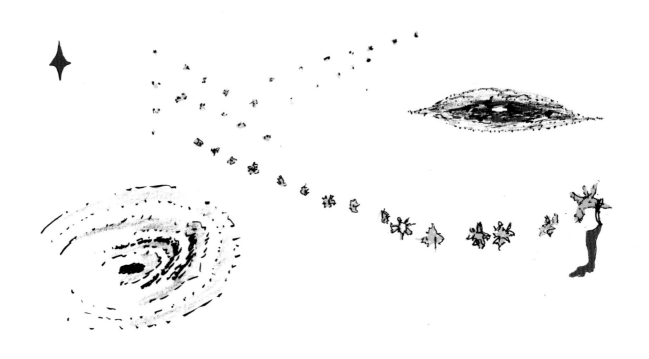

At bottom left, the earth is disappearing into a hole; top right illustrates that mysterious force 'Dark Energy'.
At bottom right is the only stocking Father Christmas can find to fill.

THE END OF THE WORLD
Predictions of the Future

Every period of history has worried about impending doom from disease, invasion by Huns, Vikings, religious oppression, Malthusian overpopulation, asteroid strike, nuclear war, famine, earthquakes, geological rifts, volcanic eruptions, Tsunamis, floods, vanishing continents, a melting earth's core and magma failure. Diseases expected to defeat humanity have included the Black Death, HIV and the Ebola virus, not forgetting that syphilis and small pox have already wiped out unprotected populations. More exotic worries have included shifts in the poles caused by invasion from space, changes in gravity, failure of the ozone layer, overheating of the planet, freezing of the planet, falling off the edge of the world, logging.

Destruction has been expected from evil forces such as the anti-Christ, witches, Zombies, Devil invaders, or space aliens. The 2000 year old list of prophesies is astonishing. Apocalyptic predictions of the Last Judgement and the end of Humanity are among the most common but astrologers, witches, sooth sayers and seers have all had their say. These have included the 16th century predictions of Nostradamus and the 18th century Joanna Southcott who believed she would give birth to a Messiah and left, after her death, a sealed wooden box of predictions which remained of enormous interest until opened 155 years later in 1927. Perhaps this was the origin of the popular phrase 'Open the Box!'

Many of these predictions have been very precise. In 1736 William Whiston said a comet would destroy Earth. In 1805, Christopher Love predicted the end of the world by Earthquake and in 1910 Flammarion foresaw that Haley's comet would snuff out all life on Earth.

Vast numbers have taken these doom laden prophecies seriously. I remember taking part in an exercise for an imminent nuclear war which would end all civilisation. So pervasive are these concerns that, today, a quarter of Britons surveyed believe the end of the world will occur during their life time.

Perhaps we should recall that humans can be more terrible than natural disaster. Religious intolerance, ethnic cleansing and death camps, which still continue today right round the world, should remind us that humans make their own disasters.

In every decade of the last 2000 years the end of the world has been predicted, so climate change protesters and 'Extinction Rebels' are just old hat. And then you have Brexit, a sure sign, apparently, of the end of everything. The only advice any politician seems able to give is that we should expect death and misery from whatever happens. We should dig a hole, or a bunker, stock up with booze and drink ourselves to death, while awaiting the end.

The end may have come to the age of the dinosaurs, but to study the history of prediction is to realise not only that there are some real nutters and credulous followers out there, but that, given the failures of so many forecasts over such a long period of time, we should have nothing to worry about. This is a good thing.

A GREAT MENHIR
The Full Stop

A menhir is a 'long stone', usually erected during the Bronze Age. I, like Obélix the menhir delivery man, have long loved the grandeur of a great stone. You can always give a menhir a good hug; this sketch is of a three metre high monolith which lives at home.

Their original purpose is uncertain. This stone is unlikely to have been a discarded glacial deposit, or to have been thrown there by giants. It may have been a marker for astronomic calculation, or the remnant of a great man's tomb, or a hill top barrow. It may have had ritual purpose and be the sole survivor of a sacred circle or the stone where young maidens were slaughtered. Or it could just be an outsized gate post.

But there is no need to worry about how it got here, since this great stone is the perfect way to bring matters to a full stop.